A Little Russian Cookbook

Tania Alexander
Vera Konnova~Stone

ILLUSTRATED BY ANNE FARRALL

First published in 1990 by
The Appletree Press Ltd,
19–21 Alfred Street, Belfast BT2 8DL
Copyright © 1990 The Appletree Press Ltd.
Illustrations © 1990 Anne Farrall used under
Exclusive License to The Appletree Press Ltd.
Printed in the EU. All rights reserved.
No part of this publication may be reproduced or transmitted in
any form or by any means, electronic or mechanical,
photocopying, recording or any information and retrieval
system, without permission in writing from the publisher.

A catalogue entry for this book is available
from the British Library.

ISBN 0-86281-254-2

First published in the United States in 1990
by Chronicle Books, 275 Fifth Street
San Francisco, CA 94103

ISBN 0-87701-798-8

10 9 8 7 6 5 4 3 2

Introduction

In the reign of Catherine the Great the culinary arts of the more advanced European countries first made their appearance in Russia. Over the two hundred years since she ruled, the Russians have given them their own exotic flavours. Because of the difficult climatic conditions in many parts of the vast Empire Russian cookery varies considerably. However, the fundamentals remain the same. Sour cream or *smetana* is used everywhere and nearly every household keeps a stock of it. Curd cheese appears extensively in desserts and sweets. Mushroom gathering is a favourite pastime in most parts of Russia, and dried mushrooms are another important ingredient of many Russian dishes. Cucumbers and beetroot are used extensively and dill is the characteristic herb. Meals usually start with *zakuski*, or hors d'oeuvres, which consist of small portions of hot or cold dishes, marinated or smoked fish, accompanied by rye bread and butter and a glass of vodka, an essential introduction to a formal meal. Russians are renowned for their hospitality and accustomed to preparing many of their dishes well in advance so they can entertain visitors and friends without difficulty.

A note on measures
Metric, imperial and volume measurements have been given for all recipes. For perfect results use one set only. Metric measures should be used where no American measure is shown, as for meat weights. Spoon measurements are level except where otherwise indicated. Seasonings can of course be adjusted according to taste. Recipes are for four.

Salat s'Krabami

Crab Salad

A salad is frequently the starter to a meal in Russia. This one makes a very good first course for a dinner party. It is one of a range of *zakuski,* or starters, a characteristic feature of the Russian table. Introduced by Peter the Great, the Europeanising and modernising Tsar, these *zakuski* show the influence of the Swedish-dominated world of the Baltic and Finland.

***

2 potatoes
1 cooking apple
½ cucumber
6 oz/170 g/1 cup crab meat, fresh or tinned
2 hard-boiled eggs
3-4 tbsp mayonnaise

***

Cook and cube potatoes. Peel, core and slice apples. Peel and dice the cucumber. Chop hard-boiled eggs. Mix with the crab meat and dress with mayonnaise.

Salat iz Sviokly

Beetroot Salad

This is another popular salad starter. Root vegetables grow well in a cold climate. Beetroot is the tastiest and most colourful, and figures in many Russian recipes.

3-4 beetroot
2 cooking apples
2 oz/50 g walnuts
2-3 cloves garlic, crushed
3-4 tbsp mayonnaise

Peel and cook the beetroot. Peel and core the apples. Grate the beetroot and the apples. Add chopped walnuts and crushed garlic and dress with mayonnaise.

Vinegret

Mixed Vegetable Salad

This is a classic starter served often with spiced pickled herrings, any kind of tinned fish or roll-mops.

---

2 medium beetroot
2 medium carrots
3 medium potatoes
½ cucumber
2-3 pickled gherkins
4 tbsp petit pois (either cooked from frozen, or tinned)
3-4 tbsp mayonnaise or French dressing

Cook beetroot, carrots and potatoes separately until just tender. Cool. Dice them, add peeled and sliced cucumber and gherkins, and cooked or tinned petit pois. Dress with mayonnaise or French dressing.

Baklazhennaya Ikra

Aubergine Caviar

This Caucasian starter is served cold with rye bread and butter and a glass of vodka. It has been popular in Russia for over 100 years.

2-3 aubergines
1 onion
2 tomatoes
parsley
salt and pepper
oil and vinegar

Place the unpeeled aubergines in the oven at gas mark 4/170°C/350°F, and bake them until soft. When cool, the skin will come off easily. Crush the flesh with a fork. Add the very finely chopped onion and finely chopped parsley. Peel and chop the tomatoes and add them to the aubergine mixture. Make a mild dressing (1 part vinegar to 3 parts oil), mix with the 'caviar' and serve cold in a glass dish.

Borshch

No two recipes are the same for borshch, but a fundamental ingredient is sour cream. It is a well known and delicious soup, particularly good when served hot on a cold winter's day. It is also refreshing served cold in summer. It should be sour-sweet and have a tang to it.

1 lb/500 g raw beetroot	salt and pepper
1 small white cabbage	1 tbsp sugar
2 pts/1 ltr/4 cups stock (beef, veal or chicken)	2 tbsps vinegar
	1 lemon
2 potatoes, diced	5 oz/125 g/1 cup sour cream

Cut the white cabbage into four. Blanch it by pouring boiling water over it. Let it stand for a few minutes with the lid on. Lift out, shred finely and pour the stock over it. Simmer. Peel the raw beetroot and cut it into matchstick-size strips, or grate it coarsely. Cook this in a separate saucepan in water and a tablespoon of vinegar for an hour. Add it with its cooking water to the cabbage soup. Add the diced potatoes, season with salt and pepper, add sugar and lemon juice to taste (or more vinegar). Simmer for 25 minutes or until beetroot is cooked. The soup should have a sharp taste. If there is too much beetroot, remove a little. It can be used as a salad. Sour cream served in a separate bowl is an essential complement.

Gribnoi Sup

Mushroom Soup

Soups are very popular in Russia, a native tradition that has never been replaced. This soup has the added advantage that its main ingredient, dried mushrooms, is available all the year round.

2 pts / 1 ltr / 4 cups meat stock	1 large carrot, sliced
2 oz / 50 g dried mushrooms	8 peppercorns
½ lb / 250 g fresh mushrooms, finely chopped	2 bay leaves
2 onions, quartered	4 oz / 100 g / ½ cup barley
1 onion, chopped	1 tbsp flour
	2 small potatoes
	2 oz / 50 g butter

Wash the dried mushrooms and soak them overnight. Use the water in which they soaked to make the stock. Fresh mushrooms can be used though the taste will be slightly different and they will not require soaking. Cook mushrooms, the quartered onions, and the carrot in the stock with peppercorns and bay leaf until soft. Take the mushrooms out of the stock. Chop them and fry with the remaining chopped onion in a little butter. Sprinkle with the flour and stir. At the same time, cook the well-washed barley in a little water. When cooked, beat it with a wooden spoon until it is creamy and white. Dice the potatoes and add these, the fried mushrooms and the creamed barley to the original bouillon. Boil for another 20 minutes until the potatoes are cooked. Season to taste.

Kholodnyi Svekolnik

Cold Beetroot Soup

Cold soups are very popular and a pleasant variation for summer, particularly this vegetarian version. This is a favourite Russian recipe.

---

1 lb/450 g beetroot
2 tbsp lemon juice
1 tbsp vinegar
1 tsp sugar (optional)
1 cucumber
2 hard-boiled eggs
2 oz/50 g spring onions
1 oz/25 g dill and parsley
5 fl oz/125 g/1 carton sour cream

Peel the beetroot and cook them in 3 pt/1 ½ ltr/6 cups water with lemon juice, vinegar and sugar. When the beetroot is tender, take it out of the liquid and cool. Grate the beetroot and return it together with sliced cucumber, chopped hard-boiled eggs and spring onion, to the strained stock. Cool for at least an hour. Garnish with chopped fresh dill and parsley, and serve with sour cream.

Rassolnik iz Diche

Game Soup with Pickles

This is one of Russia's classic soups and makes a wonderful first dinner course. It tastes even better if it is cooked on the previous day, always a help to a busy cook.

1-2 roast pheasant carcases or chicken giblets
1 potato
1 carrot
1 stick celery
2 pickled gherkins
1 oz/50 g pearl barley
salt and pepper

Make stock from the roast pheasant carcases or from chicken giblets. Strain. Add sliced potato, carrot, celery and gherkins. Cook for 25-30 minutes. Cook the pearl barley separately for 40 minutes, strain and add it to the soup. Season to taste.

Rybnaya Solyanka

Fish Soup with Pickles

This thick and filling soup is tasty, elegant, and economical. Not unlike the French bouillabaisse, it is a meal in itself.

1 lb/450 g good quality fish (salmon, halibut, or cod)	1 bay leaf
4 pickled gherkins	½ lemon
1-2 onions	salt and peppercorns
2 tomatoes or 2 tbsp tomato purée	1 tbsp capers
2 oz/50 g butter	8 stoned olives
	dill

Skin and fillet the fish. Boil the bones, head and skin in 3 pt/6 cups of water with a bay leaf, salt and peppercorns for ¾ hour. Strain this stock. Melt the butter in a heavy saucepan and fry the chopped onions lightly for 5-6 minutes. Add the fish pieces, diced gherkins, peeled and chopped tomatoes (or tomato purée) and capers. Pour hot fish stock over it. Add more seasoning if required. Cook for 10-15 minutes. Just before serving, add olives, lemon slices and some freshly chopped dill.

Rybnaya Kulebyaka

Fish Pie

Kulebyaka is a large flat pie made with delicious pastry – it can be filled with fish or meat: this recipe is for salmon. The Kulebyaka may be served hot or cold.

Pastry	Filling
8 oz/200 g cold unsalted butter	1 lb/450 g fresh salmon
1 egg	2 hard-boiled eggs
1½ oz/40 g yeast	1 medium onion
⅓ cup tepid milk	seasoning
pinch of salt	1 oz/25 g/1 tbsp butter
1 tsp sugar	
1 lb/500 g/4 cups plain flour	

Prepare the filling by poaching the salmon in seasoned water. Skin and flake the fish. Chop the hard-boiled eggs. Soften the chopped onion in the melted butter. Mix fish, eggs and onion with a little of the fish stock to bind the ingredients. To make the pastry, cut the very cold butter into small pieces. Beat the egg (saving a little for glazing) and add to the butter. Dissolve the yeast in the tepid milk and add to the butter and egg mixture. Sift the flour, sugar and salt and fold into the mixture. Knead lightly to a soft but not sticky pastry. Divide into two slightly unequal parts. Roll out the larger part to slightly overlap the baking tray. Spread the filling over it, leaving an edge of ⅔ in/15 mm. Cover with the smaller rolled-out part of the pastry. Seal the edges, prick the pastry and glaze the top with the remaining eggs (or with the milk and egg mixture). Bake in a pre-heated oven at gas mark 4/180°C/350°F for 30-40 minutes. For meat Kulebyaka make a filling of 1 lb/450 g of minced cooked beef mixed with chopped onions softened in butter and some stock. For a vegetarian filling, finely chop white cabbage and braise in butter for 25 minutes, making sure it does not brown. Season to taste and mix with two chopped hard-boiled eggs.

Rybnoye Satsivi

Fish in Georgian Walnut Sauce

Georgian recipes are very popular throughout Russia, and this sauce makes an excellent accompaniment to any cold fish dish. It can also be used with cold chicken or even game.

---

1 ½ lb / 300 g fish (usually salmon,
halibut, cod or whiting)
salt and lemon juice

Sauce

2 oz / 50 g / 4 tbsp butter	pinch of ground cloves
6 oz / 150 g walnuts	¼ tsp paprika
2 medium onions	1 small bayleaf, crushed
1 tbsp flour, rounded	½ pt / ¼ ltr / 1 cup fish stock
1 egg yolk	pinch of saffron (optional)
2-3 cloves garlic	1 oz / 25 g fresh chopped
pinch of cinnamon	parsley
	½ tsp salt

Poach the fish in salted water with some lemon juice. Remove the fish from the stock. Cool. Keep some of the stock for the sauce. To make the sauce, finely chop the onions and garlic and fry lightly in melted butter. Add flour to make a *roux*, then add the fish stock, stirring constantly. When it comes to the boil, remove from heat. Chop or grind walnuts, add them and all the other ingredients to the sauce. Mix thoroughly and leave to cool. Pour the sauce over the fish pieces and serve.

Blini

Pancakes

The week before the beginning of Lent is called Maslenitsa and it signals the end of winter. All during that week, Blini are served, signs of sun and spring.

---

1 pt/550 ml/2 cups milk, warmed
2 oz/50 g/2 tbsp yeast
10 oz/250 g/1½ cups plain flour
5 oz/125 g/½ cup buckwheat flour
2 eggs, separated
2 oz/50 g/4 tbsp butter, melted
½ tsp salt
2 ts sugar

Dissolve the yeast in one cup of tepid milk taken from the pint. Add a tsp of flour and place the mixture in a warme place. When the mixture has risen and doubled its volume, add the rest of the tepid milk, the sifted flour, sugar, salt, melted butter, and egg yolks. Beat this mixture to a very smooth batter. Place it in a warme place to rise. When the volume has doubled, knead it lightly and let it rise again. This process can be repeated once more. Add the whisked egg whites. Heat a little oil or butter in an 8-9 in frying pan and fry dollops of the mixture to make pancakes that are rather more thick than usual. Allow two or three pancakes per person and serve melted butter, sour cream, and caviar separately.

Beef Stroganoff

Alexander Grigoirevich Stroganov gave his name to this dish at the end of the last century. Whatever cut of meat is used, it must be lean. In the past, when it was not so expensive, fillet steak was recommended. However, rump or flank steak can be used if cooked slowly. Remember, the better the meat the better the results.

1½ lbs/750 g lean beef	parsley, finely chopped
2 oz/50 g/4 tbsp margarine	1 tbsp tomato purée
2 oz/50 g/4 tbsp butter	½ lb/250 g mushrooms
1 oz flour	freshly-milled black pepper
2 small onions, finely chopped	¼ pt/½ cup sour cream
½ pt/250 ml/1 cup meat stock	½ pt/250 ml/1 cup dry white wine
1 tsp mustard	

Trim and cut the meat into strips of 2 in/5 cm long and ¼ cm wide. Sprinkle the meat with salt and pepper and let it rest. In a heavy casserole make a *roux* with the margarine and flour until it turns golden brown. Slowly pour in the meat stock, stirring all the time. Bring to the boil. Add the mustard and tomato purée. Stir well. Add pepper and salt. Taste for seasoning. Set aside. Fry the onion in the butter. Add the meat strips a few at a time. Fry gently until brown. Add the onion and meat to the casserole and pour in the wine. Cook gently on the top of the stove for 1¼ hours, stirring from time to time. Wash the mushrooms well, cut finely, add to the casserole. Leave to cook for another 30 minutes. Stir in the sour cream, but do not boil. Serve, garnished with parsley, with plain rice.

Govyadina v'Smetane

Beefsteaks in Sour Cream

This is a different method of serving steak, but one which also uses sour cream to make a distinctively Russian sauce.

---

4 beefsteaks, fillet or rump
1 oz/25 g/1 tbsp dripping
salt and pepper
2 medium onions
2 oz/50 g/½ cup grated cheese
½ pt/250 ml/¾ cup sour cream

Prepare 4 trimmed steaks and brown them quickly in the frying pan with the dripping. Transfer them to a baking tray, season with salt and freshly milled pepper. Keep warm. Chop the onions and soften them in the same frying pan. Spread them over the steaks. Sprinkle with grated cheese and pour on the sour cream. Cover with foil. Bake in pre-heated oven at gas mark 4, 180°C, 350°F for an hour, removing the foil for the last 20 minutes. Serve with plain cooked vegetables.

Blinchatyi Pirog

Pancake Pie

Traditionally two kinds of filling are used in this pie: layers of cooked buckwheat and minced meat with onions and mushrooms. We prefer it with just the meat filling.

Pancakes	Filling
2 eggs	8 oz/200 g cooked minced beef
2 tbsp sugar	
¼ tsp salt	1 medium onion
½ pt/250 ml/1½ cups milk	4 oz/100 g mushrooms
4 oz/100 g/1 cup flour	1 oz/25 g/1 tbsp butter, margarine or oil
1 oz/25 g/1 tbsp melted butter, margarine or oil	

Make the filling by softening the finely chopped onion and mushrooms in the fat of your choice. Season. Mix with the cooked minced beef and leave to cool. Make pancake batter and fry 6-8 pancakes, each of 7-8 in diameter. Cover and keep them warm on a plate over boiling water. When all the pancakes are ready, put the first one in a deep baking dish, spread a layer of the meat filling, then another pancake, then more meat. Continue in this way, finishing with a pancake. Sprinkle with some melted butter and warm in the oven at gas mark 3/160°C/300°F for 15 minutes. Serve with a salad.

Pelmeni

Meat 'Ravioli'

This recipe originates in Siberia. It is said that in Siberia people prepare thousands of Pelmeni, freeze them (in cold Siberian winters you don't even need a freezer) and store them in sacks for the long winter months. Pelmeni may be cooked and eaten in a soup made from stock or as a main dish with butter or sour cream – or just with some vinegar.

Dough	Filling
2 oz/300 g/3 cups flour	6 oz/150 g minced beef
1 egg	6 oz/150 g minced pork
¼ pt/100 ml/½ cup water	1 onion
½ tsp salt	salt and pepper to taste

Sift the flour with the salt, make a well in the middle, put the egg and water into it and knead well to obtain a firm but pliable dough. Roll it out very thinly, and cut into circles with a wine glass or a 2½ in/6 cm pastry cutter. Make the filling by combining the finely minced beef and pork with the finely chopped onion. Season the mixture. Put small portions of filling onto each pastry circle and shape into crescents, sealing the edges firmly. (At this stage the Pelmeni could be frozen). Simmer them in plenty of salted water until pastry is cooked, then drain and serve with butter or sour cream. They can also be cooked in beef or chicken stock and served as a soup.

Kotletki

Russian Cutlets

Always use raw meat for this dish, an extremely popular one throughout Russia. One kind of meat can be used, but a mixture of red and white meat will make it much better. Select lean meat and ask the butcher to mince it. If mincing the meat yourself, put it through the mincer twice. Very finely minced meat will make much nicer cutlets.

¾ lb/350 g lean beef (chuck steak or flank)	a little margarine or oil
	parsley
¾ lb/350 g shin of pork or veal	I egg
	breadcrumbs or flour
4 oz/100 g/4 slices stale white bread	salt and pepper
	½ cup sour cream
I onion	

Remove the crust from the slices of bread, break into pieces and soak them in plenty of cold water. Chop the onion finely and fry it in the oil or margarine. Chop the parsley. Take a large bowl and mix the two minced meats together, add the well-squeezed-out bread, fried onion, parsley, egg, salt and pepper. Add a little cold water to make the mixture moist and soft. Mix well. Sprinkle a wooden board with a little flour or breadcrumbs. Dip a tablespoon in cold water to keep the mixture from sticking, lift out a portion, roll it into a ball, roll in the flour, flatten a little. Do the same for each cutlet. Fry in very hot oil or margarine for 5 minutes on each side. Turn the heat to very low and cook the cutlets slowly for another 10 minutes. Remove them from the pan. Add a little sour cream to the oil and pour the sauce over the cutlets. Serve either hot or cold with rice or mashed potatoes.

Ris s'Loukom

Rice with Onion

There are many ways of cooking rice. The advantage of this method is that it does not require attention at the last moment.

---

1 cup long grain rice
2½ cups water
1 onion
2 oz/50 g margarine
salt

Bring the water, chopped onion and salt to the boil. Toss the rice in the margarine in a frying pan, stirring all the time, until it is transparent. Transfer the rice to a heavy fireproof dish, pour the strained boiling water over it. Cover. Place in the oven and cook until the liquid is absorbed and the grains are separated (about 20 minutes). The rice will not spoil if cooked much longer in a very low oven.

Kartofelynie Kotlety s'Gribnym Sousom

Potato Cakes with Mushroom Sauce

Potatoes were introduced to Russia in the late eighteenth century. Many Russian potato dishes show the influence of French and German cuisine. This one makes a very good vegetarian main dish.

1 lb/450 g potatoes	1 egg
2 oz/50 g/2 tbsp margarine	2 oz/50 g/½ cup flour

Sauce

4 oz/100 g mushrooms	1 tbsp flour
6 fl oz/½ ltr/1½ cups stock made with a vegetable stock cube	1 onion
	4 oz/100 g/4 tbsp margarine

Cook the potatoes, drain thoroughly and mash while still hot. Mix well with 2 tbsp of margarine, an egg, and flour. Form into flat round rissoles. Roll them in flour or breadcrumbs. Fry in very hot fat. Keep warm while you make the sauce. To make the sauce, wash and slice the mushrooms. Finely chop the onion and fry it gently in 2 tbsp margarine. In a separate pan melt another 2 tbsp margarine and add flour. Slowly pour the vegetable stock into the mixture, stirring all the time, and cook gently for 5 minutes. Add the fried mushrooms and onion. Season to taste and serve with the potato cakes.

Tushennaya Markov

Braised Carrots

Russians look on carrots as a sweet vegetable and, characteristically, recipes tend to enhance the natural sugar content. Cooking the carrots with sugar adds as piquancy to their taste.

1 lb/450 g carrots
2 tbsp butter
1 tsp sugar
2 tsp flour
salt

Cut the carrots lengthways into 1½ in strips. Almost cover with boiling water and add salt. Add a tablespoon of butter. Simmer for 20-30 minutes. Mix another tablespoon of butter with the flour. Add to the carrots and stir for a few minutes. Add the sugar. Boil for 5-10 minutes until the liquid is nearly evaporated.

Krassnaya Kapusta

Red Cabbage

Cabbage is a very versatile vegetable in the Russian kitchen and in poorer households can be a replacement for meat or fish. However, this dish is also an excellent accompaniment to any roast meat.

---

1 medium red cabbage
1 onion, finely chopped
2 tbsp vinegar
1 tbsp brown sugar
2 apples
salt and pepper
a little oil
1 cup water

Wash and shred the cabbage finely, discard core and coarse leaves. Fry the onion in a little oil in a heavy casserole, then add the cabbage. Stir for a few minutes, add a cup of water, the vinegar, sugar, salt and pepper and the cut-up apples. Bring to the boil. Reduce heat and cook very slowly for 1½-2 hours.

Grechnevaya Kasha

Cooked Buckwheat

Kasha is served as an alternative to rice with any meat dish. It is delicious by itself with butter. 'Cabbage soup and buckwheat are our main foods' is an old Russian saying. Traditionally, cold kasha was eaten with milk at breakfast.

---

8 oz/200 g/2 cups buckwheat
1½ pts/¾ ltr/3 cups water
¾ tsp salt
2 tbsp butter

Pour boiling salted water over the washed buckwheat in a heavy saucepan. Skim off any grains which rise to the top. Add butter and cook for 25-30 minutes until the water has evaporated. Cover tightly with a cloth and lid. Leave for 3-4 hours. Alternatively, Kasha may be cooked in an ovenproof dish in the oven at gas mark 2/160°C/300°F for 2 hours. Stir it with a fork from time to time. Serve with a knob of butter. Like rice, the grains should remain separated. The Kasha can be reheated and used the next day.

Tvorozhnaya Zapekanka

Curd Cheese Pudding

This is quite easy to prepare. It is not too sweet and therefore very versatile. On its own this can make a good light supper dish.

---

1 lb/450 g curd cheese
1 egg
3 tbsp sour cream
3 tbsp sugar
2 tbsp semolina
4 oz/100 g/⅔ cup sultanas
knob of butter or margarine
1 dsp cake or biscuit crumbs

Mix all ingredients thoroughly except sultanas (an electric mixer will make it easier). Add sultanas. Grease a soufflé dish and sprinkle it with cake or biscuit crumbs. Put the mixture into the dish. A little sour cream or melted butter may be spread on the top. Bake in the oven at gas mark 5/190°C/375°F for 30 minutes. Serve with any fruit sauce.

Kulich

Easter Cake

The cooking of the Easter cake, which is considered the focal test of a Russian woman's culinary skills, is surrounded by many legends. It is only undertaken once a year but most households bake several Kulich for their own consumption and to give away to friends and relatives. There are many recipes for the cake. This is a relatively simple one which nevertheless takes some time to complete. The traditional cake should look like a chef's hat, narrow and high, but it may be difficult to find a suitable tin.

2 eggs	1 lb/450 g/3 cups plain flour
7 fl oz/200 g/1 cup tepid milk	2 oz/50 g/⅓ cup sultanas
6 oz/150 g/1 cup sugar	1 oz/25 g mixed peel
2 oz/50 g/1 tbsp yeast	pinch of salt
4 oz/100 g/½ cup unsalted melted butter	a few drops of vanilla essence
	a little oil

Dissolve the yeast in tepid milk, add sugar, eggs, melted butter and mix well, using an electric mixer if available. Leave the mixture in a warm place for 4 hours to let the dough ferment and rise slightly. Fold in the flour, add the sultanas, peel, salt and vanilla and knead well with oiled hands. Kneading is important. Grease a 9 in/23 cm cylindrical cake tin and line it with greased greaseproof paper. The paper should protrude at least 6 in/15 cm above the top of the tin. Put the dough into the tin and leave it for another hour. This second rising must take place in the cake tin. Pre-heat the oven to gas mark 4/180°C/350°F and bake for 45 minutes. Test to see if cooked. The day before eating, make a little icing (icing sugar and white of egg), pour it over the cake to drop down like candle-grease. Cut the cake in rounds as needed, replacing the iced top to keep the rest of the cake fresh.

Limonnyi Pirog

Lemon Tarts

This is a very simple and quick recipe for a delicious pudding or a tea-time treat.

Pastry
(as for Kulebyaka, *see page 23)*
Filling
1 large whole lemon
6 oz/75 g/1½ cups sugar
beaten egg for brushing

Grate the whole lemon, discarding any pips. Mix with sugar. Divide the pastry into two parts, one slightly larger than the other, and roll them out. Place the larger part on a baking tray and spread the lemon filling on it. Cover with the smaller square, pressing the edges firmly down. Brush the top with a little of the beaten egg and prick with a fork. Bake in the oven at gas mark 5/190°C/375°F. Cut into squares and serve hot with cream. The tarts can also be eaten cold.

Pashka

Easter Dessert

'Pashka' means Easter, and this is the main Easter dish. It must be in the shape of a pyramid, as large or as small as you wish. In Russia there were special wooden moulds for making Pashka. They were embossed with Christian symbols such as X.B., which stands for 'Christ is risen', or with the Russian Orthodox cross. The rich, sweet Pashka is eaten with the Kulich, the light, dry Easter cake. This recipe requires no cooking.

4 oz/100 g/½ cup unsalted butter, softened	*4 oz/100 g/⅔ cup sultanas*
6 oz/150 g sugar	*2 oz/50 g chopped almonds*
2 egg yolks	*few drops vanilla essence*
1 lb/450 g curd cheese	*1 oz/25 g chopped peel*
2 oz/50 g/2 tbsp double cream	

Beat together the butter and sugar. Add the egg yolks, curd cheese and cream. Mix well to a creamy consistency. Add the almonds, vanilla essence, sultanas and peel to the mixture. Place it in a well-washed earthenware flower-pot lined with muslin, or in a tall plastic container with holes in the bottom. Stand the pot or container in a bowl to catch the excess liquid. Allow the mixture to settle into the shape of the pot or container. Fold the muslin over the top of the pot. Put a plate with a heavy weight on top of the pot and leave it in the fridge overnight. Turn out before serving and place coloured hard-boiled eggs around it.

Kissel

Fruit Purée

Not unlike blancmange, Kissel probably arrived in Russia at the same time. This classic Russian sweet is usually made with blackcurrants or cranberries, but any other soft fruit can be used. Be careful not to overthicken it.

1½ tbsp arrowroot or cornflour
2 x 13 oz/350 g tins of blackcurrants in their own juice or
1½ lb/1 kg fresh fruit
1 tbsp golden syrup
water

Put the blackcurrants and their juice into a fine sieve over a saucepan. Gently press the berries through the sieve, throwing away the remaining pulp. Stir the purée into the juice in the saucepan and add the golden syrup. Add water to bring the liquid to 1½ pints/¾ ltr/3 cups. If you are using fresh fruit, bring to the boil with a little water and a little sugar, then proceed as above. Mix the arrowroot with a little water to make a smooth paste. Boil the juice and fruit and gradually add it to the arrowroot paste stirring all the time. Transfer all back to the saucepan. Cook on a low heat for 5 minutes stirring all the time to prevent lumps. Pour into individual dishes while hot. Place in refrigerator when cool to set. Serve with cream.

Vatrushki

Curd Cheese Tartlets

Russians enjoy with tea all kinds of sweet pastry made with fillings of fruit or curd cheese. The latter are called Vatrushki – the very sound of the word is cosy and comforting.

Pastry

1½ oz/40 g/1 tbsp yeast	1½ lb/600 g/6 cups flour
¼ pt/½ cup tepid milk	1 egg
4 oz/100 g/½ cup sugar	2 oz/50 g/2 tbsp butter
10 oz/250 g/¾ cup single cream	softened
	3 tbsp oil

Filling

1 lb/450 g curd cheese	4 oz/100 g/½ cup sugar
2 eggs	

Dissolve yeast in the tepid milk, add 2 tbsp sugar and 2 tbsp flour taken from the recommended amount. Mix and put in a warm place to rise. When doubled, add cream and half the flour. Put back into a warm place to rise. Beat an egg well with the remaining sugar, softened butter and oil. Mix with the risen dough and add the remaining flour. Knead well and leave to rise. Then knead lightly once or twice. Turn the dough onto a surface sprinkled with flour and divide into small rolls. Leave to rest for a few minutes. Mix the filling ingredients to a smooth substance. Flatten each roll into a circle 2 in/5 cm in diameter. Put a tablespoon of the filling in the middle of each circle and shape them into open tartlets. Brush with milk and place on an oiled baking tray 1 in/2½ cm apart. Bake in a pre-heated oven at gas mark 4/180°C/350°F.

Index